A Guide For Beginners

HOW TO SELL LIKE CRAZY ON FACEBOOK MARKETPLACE

CHIKA NJOKU

How to sell like crazy on Facebook Marketplace

Written by Chika Njoku

© Copyright Chika Njoku 2021- All rights reserved.

The content contained within this book may not be reproduced, duplicated, or transmitted without direct written permission from the author or the publisher.

Under no circumstances will any blame or legal responsibility be held against the publisher, or author, for any damages, reparation, or monetary loss due to the information contained within this book. Either directly or indirectly. You are responsible for your own choices, actions, and results.

Legal Notice:

This book is copyright protected. This book is only for personal use. You cannot amend, distribute, sell, use, quote or paraphrase any part, or the content within this book, without the consent of the author or publisher.

Disclaimer Notice:

Please note the information contained within this document is for educational and entertainment purposes only. All effort has been executed to present accurate, up to date, and reliable, complete information. No warranties of any kind are declared or implied. Readers acknowledge that the author is not engaging in the rendering of legal, financial, medical, or professional advice. The content within this book has been derived from various sources. Please consult a licensed professional before attempting any techniques outlined in this book.

By reading this document, the reader agrees that under no circumstances is the author responsible for any losses, direct or indirect, which are incurred as a result of the use of the information contained within this document, including, but not limited to, — errors, omissions, or inaccuracies.

Dedication

A big thanks goes to my lovely husband, Charles, who also took the pain to review, edit and proof-read this book. A massive thanks also to my lovely kids, Michael, David and Sophie for their huge support, encouragement and understanding. You all made this happen. I love you all.

Table of Contents:

Contents

CHAPTER 1	7
Section 1.1 : About Facebook	9
Section 1.2: Why is Facebook So Popular?	10
Chapter 2	11
Section 2.1: What is Facebook Marketplace?	11
Section 2.2: How do I get Facebook Marketplace?	12
Section 2.3: Is Facebook Marketplace Free?	12
Section 2.4 : How to start selling on Facebook Market Place	13
Section 2.5: How to list an item on Facebook Marketplace	13
Chapter 3	16
Section 3.1: How to know when Buyers want your listed Product(s)	16
Section 3.2 : Payment Method	16
Chapter 4	17
Section 4.1: What to sell on your Facebook Marketplace?	17
Section 4.2: How to source for what you want to sell	18
Chapter 5	19
Section 5.1: What to do if your item isn't selling on the Facebook Marketplace?	19
Chapter 6	20
Section 6.1: How to sell on Facebook Marketplace without friends seeing?	20
Chapter 7	21
Section 7.1: Renewal of listing	21
Section 7.2: How to Renew Your Listing on Marketplace?	21
Section 7.3: Facebook Marketplace Menu	22

Section 7.4: View Messages on Facebook Marketplace ... 23

Section 7.5: How do I edit my listing on Facebook Marketplace? ... 23

Section 7.6: When to Mark your listing as Sold ... 24

Section 7.7: Steps on how to mark your listing as sold: ... 24

Section 7.8: When to Mark your listing as Pending ... 24

Section 7.9: Steps on How to Mark an Item as Pending ... 25

Section 7.10: When to Mark your listing as Available ... 25

Section 7.11: Steps on How to Mark an item as Available ... 25

Section 7.12: How do I delete my listing on Facebook Marketplace? ... 26

Chapter 8 ... 27

Section 8.1: How to build your Seller Rank on Facebook Marketplace ... 27

Section 8.2: How to Rate a Seller or Buyer? ... 27

Section 8.3: How to see Your Ratings as a Seller on Marketplace ... 27

Section 8.4: Top tips for Facebook Marketplace Sellers ... 28

CHAPTER 9 ... 29

Section 9.1: Facebook Market Regulations ... 29

Section 9.2: Do I need a business license to sell on Facebook? ... 30

Section 9.3: How to Set Up a Shop Section on Your Facebook Page ... 30

Chapter 10 ... 31

Section 10.1: Conclusion ... 31

Resources ... 32

Dear Friend,

Your decision to purchase this guidebook on 'How to Sell Like Crazy on Facebook Marketplace' may turn out to be one of the smartest decisions you have made.

Many of us are on the move to make some extra money, we've either set the plans on how to pay off our debts, phone bill, credit cards bill, or we simply want to make a few extra Money.

But where does the extra money come from?

What do you do when you do not have the time for a second job but need more money to pay the bills?

If you are looking for a way to make some relatively easy money while also cleaning your house out, you have come to the right place.

In this guidebook, you will learn some ways of making money just by using any of your devices such as Laptops, phones, or tablets.

Having used Facebook Marketplace for several years and generated huge income from the platform, I will be showing you some guides on how you can also make money by selling on the platform.

In this guidebook, I will be revealing to you the exact step by step process I follow every time I list my items for sale on Facebook Marketplace.

I will also be giving you some top ideas where you can source items you want to list for sales on Facebook Marketplace.

CHAPTER 1

Introduction

You have chosen this guidebook because you think it can help you get more money through Facebook Marketplace. You are on the right part as they say, 'no information is too small'.

I had my Facebook opened in 2008 just for socializing and posting my pictures and making and meeting new friends, just like most people. When Facebook introduced their marketplace, I never understood how and what happens there, so I never gave it a trial.

Fast forward to 2017, One day, I was just playing around with my phone, and I decided to open the Marketplace item to really see what was happening there and I saw so many items listed by so many people for sale and I saw that It had options for anyone to just add photos straight away without any joining cost, etc. So, I decided to look at the top picked items to have an idea on what people really wanted. I did that for so many days just trying to really understand the top pick trends on the Facebook Marketplace.

The next step was to find out where to get the items that I wanted to list for sale. In this Guidebook I will also be giving you some ideas on how to source for items you want to list for sale.

I was excited to start this new journey on Facebook Marketplace when I got my first product. I made sure I took good quality pictures and followed all the steps I will be sharing with you in this guidebook and went ahead to list my items.

I was so surprised on the huge demands I got that I sold off all items in less than 48 hours. That was so insane!

So, everything I am about to teach you works! You only need to have a device and a Facebook Account, and you can make serious money working from home.

There are so many ways you can make money on Facebook:
- By being a Social Media influencer
- Affiliate Marketing
- Develop an app
- Selling on Facebook Marketplace.

For the sole purpose of this guidebook, we will be looking at the selling on Facebook Marketplace as one of the ways of making money on Facebook.

Let us dive in!

Section 1.1: **About Facebook**

According to Wikipedia, Facebook is An American Online social networking service company based in Menlo Park at California.

Facebook was founded by Mark Zuckerberg along with his fellow roommates at Harvard College in 2004.

Facebook is one of the worlds most valuable companies and considered as one of the Big five companies in Information Technology Industry just like Google, Apple, Amazon and Microsoft.

Facebook Offers Products and services beyond its social networking platform, including Facebook Messenger, Facebook Watch and Facebook Portal.

It also acquired Instagram, WhatsApp, Oculus VR, Giphy and Mapillary.

Section 1.2: <u>Why is Facebook So Popular?</u>

Facebook is a website which allows users, to sign up for free socializing profiles to connect with friends, work colleagues, or people they do not know, online. It allows users to share pictures, videos, music and so much more.

Many uses it for social networking because Facebook gives people control over what they share, who they share it with, the content they see and experience

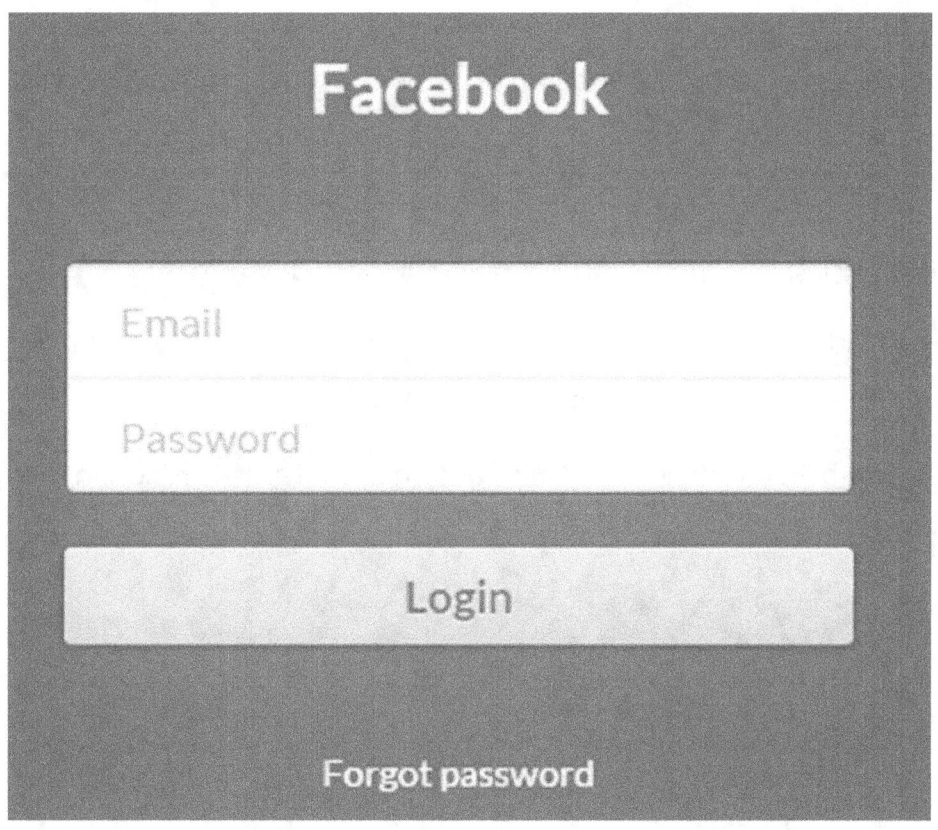

Chapter 2

Section 2.1: <u>What is Facebook Marketplace?</u>

Facebook Marketplace is an online platform for users to buy and sell goods locally or shipped through Facebook.

Facebook Marketplace icon is found in your Facebook Feed Menu.

This guidebook is for you if you want to learn how to make money by selling locally on Facebook Marketplace.

One of my best ways of making money from home is by selling on Facebook Marketplace. Now, with the new norm of working from home due to the Covid19 Pandemic, this is the best time to turn all those stuffs lying around your home both new and used items into cash.

You can make good money selling good items on Facebook Marketplace.

Whether you are selling, advertising, or marketing on Facebook you need to know how to make money on Facebook using your phone, tablet, laptop, or desktop.

Facebook is used by over two billion people worldwide and more than 214 million in the United States alone.

Section 2.2: How do I get Facebook Marketplace?

Marketplace is available on the Facebook app which you can access with your phones, Laptops, Desktops, and Tablets.

On different phones, the Marketplace icon are located differently.

Example, Samsung phones (Androids) have the Facebook Marketplace icon on the top menu, while iPhones (IOS) have theirs on the lower part of the menu.

If you are using a Laptop to browse, you can find this Marketplace icon on the left side of the Facebook page.

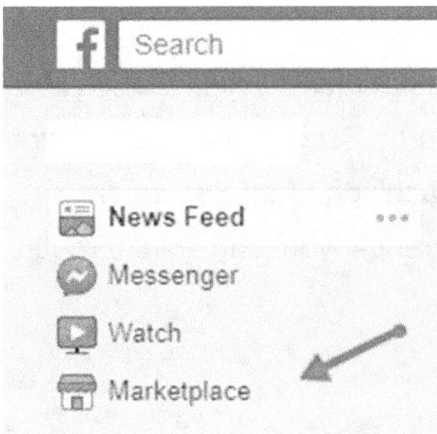

Section 2.3: Is Facebook Marketplace Free?

Yes, Facebook Marketplace is free.

No setup cost, No administration fees, No joining fee, No listing fee, etc.

You can sell items on Facebook Marketplace for no fee, and the process to list your items only takes a few minutes.

Section 2.4: How to start selling on Facebook Market Place

Step 1: You must have access to a device with internet network. For example, Phone, Tablet, Laptop or Desktop.

Step 2. You must have a Facebook account to be able to do so.

If you do not have an account with Facebook, then you can create one (It is easy and free too!).

Once you have created your account on Facebook, the marketplace icon is on the left side bar menu if you are using a laptop.

Now we are ready to start selling on Facebook Marketplace.

Before you can sell an item on Marketplace, you must create a public listing that can be seen by anyone on and off Facebook. This includes people on Facebook groups, News Feed, Marketplace, Facebook search engines and other places on or off Facebook. You can also choose to post your listings to many other groups you can join through Facebook Marketplace, like any Buy and Sell Groups.

Section 2.5: How to list an item on Facebook Marketplace

Step 1: From your Facebook News Feed, go to the Marketplace Icon,

Step 2: Click on the 'Sell' button. Once this is done, 'Create New Listing' option will pop up with different options (Example: Items, Vehicles, Jobs, etc.)

Let us assume you want to sell a female dress on Facebook Marketplace, you will click the item listing options where it will ask you for the next step.

Step 3

- **Add Photos**: (Make sure you take many super quality pictures of your product showing them from diver's angles.)
- **Tittle**: Write a title to describe what you are selling.
- **Price**: Write the price you want to sell your product. **So always consider the right price to attract customers/ buyers.**

    Also note that people want to buy great quality and lovely items at a very good, sometimes low price.

    You can include postage cost in your price. This is optional, but make sure to communicate that postage cost is included already in the price.
- **Category**: A drop down menu button will show you all the categories available for selection (Baby & Children, Clothing & accessories, etc.)

As you create your listing, bear in mind that there are about 30 categories to choose from when you are creating a listing on Marketplace. For Instance, Baby & Kids, Furniture, Tools, Toys & Games, Vehicles, Rentals, etc.

Categorizing your item properly helps customers/buyers to find your product when searched.

So, for example, if you want to sell a female dress on Facebook Marketplace, you will select the 'Clothing and Accessories' category which has 'Women's Clothing & Shoes' as sub-category.

- **Condition:** You need to let your customers know the condition of the product (Example, if the item is New, Used, etc.) Select the best condition of the item from the drop menu.
- **Location:** Your location is also needed so people near you can check out what you are selling, while those far from your location can contact you to discuss/arrange how the item can be dispatched to them.
- **Description**: Write a full, honest description of the item you want to sell. For example, Color and size of the dress you want to sell.

- **Tags**: This is optional. But very good to make your listing show up when customers are searching for items in that category.
  Example, you can tag your product as evening dress, etc. (whatever keywords you feel people will search for on Facebook Marketplace to find it.

Step 4

- Next, is the Publish button!

Here, your item will be reviewed by a Facebook Administrator just to make sure it meets the marketplace requirements and conditions of selling. Once the Admin is happy, the product is approved, and you are live, ready for customers to find your product.

Facebook Marketplace review can take between 5 minutes to 2 days for approval depending on the fulfillment of the terms and conditions of selling. But most times, they are reviewed under 5 minutes if no issues are found.

Chapter 3

Section 3.1: How to know when Buyers want your listed Product(s)

Once your product goes live, Customers who are interested in your listing will send you a message which comes up as notification on your Facebook Messenger.

'Is it available'?

This can be customized to the template of words you prefer to use from the settings section. For example, a potential buyer can change the 'Is it available' template to 'Is this item still available'? Or use any word(s) that suits him or her.

So, once you get your Facebook Messenger notification of interest from your potential buyer, you both can talk more about the product, agree on the price, payment option and pickup location or postage details.

Section 3.2: Payment Method

Your customer might want to know your payment options, postage cost, delivery options, etc.

Most preferred payment options for people who are locally based include cash, PayPal or Revolut transfer.

For others, who are not locally based, different payment methods are agreed by both parties. For example (Bank Transfers, Postal Orders, Revolut Transfers, etc.)

Note, always be careful with the transactions to be shipped. Sellers can fall into the wrong hands. Always ask for payment proof so you can validate the payments before posting/shipping items to Customers.

Chapter 4

Section 4.1: What to sell on your Facebook Marketplace?

It depends on what level you want to do on the marketplace, you can sell your personal stuff you do not need anymore, or you can sell brand new stuff as a retailer (Large quantities).

For example, you can sell used or brand-new items like Laptops, phones, television, etc. If you are just selling out your unwanted stuff, these can also be sold on Facebook marketplace. You can also sell large quantities of basic needs that people want.

Examples of what you can sell on Facebook Marketplace.

- Earphones
- Smart Watches
- Video Games Consoles
- Women Dresses
- Men Dresses
- Footwears
- Children Wears
- Phones

You need to do your research to see what people really need/want if you want to sell brand new stuff (wholesale) as a retailer.

Section 4.2: <u>How to source for what you want to sell</u>

- There are plenty online sites that can help you connect with manufacturers of various products around the world. So do some online research and be careful of unreliable suppliers and scammers.
- Find potential Suppliers and attend their event /Trade shows. It's important you connect with suppliers and ask questions.

Some Recommended Online sites you can contact manufacturers or buy from are:

- Amazon (So many top manufacturers are there, do your research)
- Dhgate
- Aliexpress
- Alibaba

Make sure to sample out quality of products before you get your big orders.

Chapter 5

Section 5.1: What to do if your item isn't selling on the Facebook Marketplace?

1. **There may be no demand for what you are selling**: You can join more Marketplace groups so you can list your items to get more audience.
2. **The price may be too high**: you can reduce your price just to see if that will help.

Customers are always looking out for bargains and will be interested in your items when they feel your price is worth the item value.

If still having low sales or no response, you can consider boosting your listing for a small fee. (This is for those ready to pay for adverts for their listings).

The budget you want to spend on your Facebook boost is totally up to you! You simply enter the total amount you want to spend, and Facebook will spread it evenly across the duration you choose. The average minimum cost of a boost is $1 per day, and that is in your local currency too.

To boost your listing:

- Open the items you listed on Marketplace.
- Click Boost Listing.
- Set your total budget.
- Choose how long your ad will run.
- Choose your payment method.
- Preview your boosted listing.
- Click Boost Listing.

But from my experience selling on Facebook Marketplace with highly rated badges, Boosting is a No for me. I have tried it and it did not work for me. However, this does not mean that it does not work.

You can try finding the right items in demand for your buyers to avoid spending money on boosting your listing.

Chapter 6

Section 6.1: How to sell on Facebook Marketplace without friends seeing?

Many people are skeptical to sell stuff on Facebook because they are worried about their friends seeing what they are selling.

If you want to sell items on Facebook Marketplace without friends seeing, easily select "Hide from friends" under the privacy settings. This will hide the listing from your Facebook friends but go on to be visible to other people on Facebook

While Marketplace items can be seen by anyone on or off Facebook, you can change your privacy settings when creating your listing.

.

Choose Privacy Settings

🔒 **Hide from friends**
This listing will be hidden from your Facebook friends but visible to other people on Facebook.

Marketplace items are public and can be seen by anyone on or off Facebook. Items like animals, drugs, weapons, counterfeits, and other items that infringe intellectual property aren't allowed on Marketplace. See our **Commerce Policies**.

Chapter 7

Section 7.1: <u>Renewal of listing</u>

You can renew your listing every week with a maximum of 5 times per item

Section 7.2: <u>How to Renew Your Listing on Marketplace?</u>

To renew your listing on Facebook Marketplace for more visibility, your listing must have been live on the platform for at least 7 days (a week) for the renew button to be active for you to be able to renew your items.

Steps to Renew your Listing:

- Go to your Listing on Facebook Marketplace
- Select your items you want to renew from your listing
- Click on Manage from the menu on your screen
- Click Renew in Marketplace

Section 7.3: Facebook Marketplace Menu

This is a snip from my Facebook Marketplace Menu.

I will be explaining the step-by-step guide on how each menu can be used.

- 💬 View Messages
- 📧 View listing
- 🗑 Delete listing
- ✏️ Edit listing
- ✅ Mark as sold
- ⏸ Mark as pending
- 🚀 Boost Listing
- 👥 List in more places
- ➡️ Share listing

Section 7.4: View Messages on Facebook Marketplace

This option allows you to see all the messages you got from all your listed items.

For Example, most notifications of interest from your buyers comes up as a messenger chat, but you can go to your menu to see on different items various messages.

This is so helpful when you have volumes of messages from your buyers due to huge demand especially when you have multiple items listed for sale.

To see Messages with buyers or sellers on Marketplace:

- Open the Facebook app and tap Menu (3 Lines)
- Scroll down and click on Marketplace .Click on more if you cant see the Icon
- Tap at the top
- Select Inbox.

Section 7.5: How do I edit my listing on Facebook Marketplace?

Here are the steps to follow:

- From your News Feed, Select Marketplace.
- Go to Your Account.
- Click on Your Listings.
- Go to the listing you want to edit.
- Select Edit Listing.
- Edit your item's details and then Select Update.

Section 7.6: When to Mark your listing as Sold

When a sale has been made, you can mark a listing as sold.

After you mark the listing as sold, it will no longer be visible to anyone else on Marketplace. All buyers/Customers who messaged you about the item will get a message saying that the item has been sold.

Section 7.7: <u>Steps on how to mark your listing as sold</u>:

- From your News Feed, Go to Marketplace.
- Go to Your Account.
- Go on to the Listings.
- Select Mark As... on the listing you want to edit.
- Select Mark as Sold.

After you mark the item as sold, the buyer/Purchaser of the item will receive a notification to rate you as a seller.

Section 7.8: <u>When to Mark your listing as Pending</u>

You can mark a listing as pending when you have settled to sell the item to a buyer/ Customer, but the sale is not completed yet.

All buyers/ who have messaged you about the listing will get a notification saying that the item is pending. New buyers/Customers will see that the sale is pending before they can message you.

Section 7.9: <u>Steps on How to Mark an Item as Pending</u>

- From your News Feed, go to Marketplace.
- Go to Your Account.
- Go to the Listings.
- Select Mark As... on the listing you want to edit.
- Select Mark as Pending.

Section 7.10: When to Mark your listing as Available

If you marked a listing as sold or pending, you can change it back to available. Buyers/Customers who messaged you about the listing before will get a message saying that the item is now available. Those Messenger communications will be unarchived if the listing was previously marked as sold.

Section 7.11: Steps on How to Mark an item as Available

- From your News Feed, click Marketplace.
- Go to Your Account.
- Select the Listing.
- Go to Mark As... on the listing you want to edit.
- Select Mark as Available.

Section 7.12: How do I delete my listing on Facebook Marketplace?

To delete your Marketplace listing:

- From your News Feed, Select Marketplace in the top left.
- Go to Your Account.
- Select Your Listings.
- Go to the listing you want to delete.
- Select Delete, then click Delete again.

Chapter 8

Section 8.1: <u>How to build your Seller Rank on Facebook Marketplace</u>

Buyers and Sellers who have interacted with each other on Facebook Marketplace can rate themselves. So, to build your sellers rank, you need to be:

- Be friendly: Good and excellent communication with your customers at all time
- Be completely Honest with your buyers/customers at all time.

- Be active, responsive, and professional: If you can reply to messages about your items within an hour, you can earn the "Very Responsive" badge and your typical response time is listed on your profile.
- Punctuality: Be on time with Customers for meet up.
- Make sure the price is right.
- Mark your item as sold whenever they are sold.

Section 8.2: How to Rate a Seller or Buyer?

On your Facebook messenger chat/ conversation group with your buyer, tap on the customer profile, options of ratings will come up and you can select to rate a buyer

Select a happy face or a sad face.

Section 8.3: How to see Your Ratings as a Seller on Marketplace

Go to your commerce profile and look for the 'Ratings as a Seller' section. You can swipe left to see their Ratings as a Buyer. People can choose to make their ratings as a buyer or a seller private.

Section 8.4: Top tips for Facebook Marketplace Sellers

- Make sure that your item follows Facebook's Commerce Policies before listing anything for Product/Item sale.
- Never ship an item before you receive full payment. You can request for proof of payment and do your part to validate the proof of payment. Example, the buyer can send you slip of payment for a bank transfer as proof.

- Clearly communicate the shipping timeline, delivery status and tracking information to your buyer. (I always tell my customers that local postage takes 1-3 working days for them to receive goods, once payment is received.)
- Consider using a payment option that provides purchase protection, Example PayPal.

CHAPTER 9

Section 9.1: Facebook Market Regulations

Make sure you review and adhere to Facebook Commerce Policies before selling your products/items on Facebook Marketplace, these policies will help you understand what items can and cannot be sold on Facebook.

Facebook market have some prohibited items they do not approve on their platform.

Some examples of items that are not allowed on Facebook Marketplace include:

- Ingestible supplements
- Adult products and services
- Real money gambling services
- Digital products or subscriptions
- Ammunition, Weapons, or explosives
- Animals
- Prescription, Illegal or recreational drugs
- Tobacco products
- Virtual, Real, or fake currency

Facebook can reject your item if they feel it is an item on their rejected list. You can submit an appeal and if they do not approve the listing, you just must delete it and try again.

But most times, they approve the listing once they review and see it is not on their rejected list.

Section 9.2 Do I need a business license to sell on Facebook.

No, you do not need a business license or tax registration to sell on Facebook Marketplace. You can file for taxes using your social security number. Many people do not like having their social security number hovering around these days so applying for an EIN (Tax ID) number is an alternative.

Section 9.3: How to Set Up a Shop Section on Your Facebook Page

- Discover how to set up a Shop section on your Facebook page.
- Look for the 'Add Shop' Section link below your cover photo.
- Click the 'Add Shop' Section button.
- Agree to the Merchant Terms and Policies.
- Enter business details and set up payment processing.
- The call-to-action button changes to Shop Now.

Please leave a Review if you enjoyed this!

I will be incredibly thankful if you can take 60 seconds of your precious time to write a brief review for me on Amazon, even if it is just few sentences, thank you!

Chapter 10

Section 10.1 Conclusion

How to use Facebook Marketplace: A Summary step-by-step guide.

Step 1 When you log in to Facebook you should notice a new 'shop' icon Marketplace

Step 2 Click on the Marketplace Icon, then you will be prompted by Facebook to add a photo of the item you are selling. When adding photos, take multiple high-quality photos showing different angles

Step 3 Add a Title to the item you want to list.

Step 4 Add a detailed description of the item you want to list.

Step 5 Set a price for your item.

Step 6 Add your location to let people closer to you find your product.

Step 7 Chose a product Category for your product.

Step 8 Publish your listing.

Step 9 You are Live on Facebook Marketplace ready to start selling

If you want to hear more on how to make money on Facebook Marketplace, please feel free to email

Resources

- Facebook Marketplace. (2021). Https://Www.Facebook.Com/Marketplace. https://www.facebook.com/marketplace
- Help Center, F. (2021). Using Facebook. Https://Www.Facebook.Com/Help/1680504982210398. https://www.facebook.com/help/1680504982210398

- How to Make Money with Facebook Marketplace. (2020). Earlymorningmoney. https://www.earlymorningmoney.com/how-to-make-money-with-facebook-marketplace/
- W. (2020). Facebook, Inc. Wikipedia. https://en.wikipedia.org/wiki/Facebook,_Inc.
- W.E.B.W.I.S.E. (2021). What is Facebook? Https://Www.Webwise.Ie/Parents/Explained-What-Is-Facebook-2/. https://www.webwise.ie/parents/explained-what-is-facebook-2/

www.ingramcontent.com/pod-product-compliance
Lightning Source LLC
Chambersburg PA
CBHW082025230526
45466CB00023B/3593